PLATFORM PAPERS

QUARTERLY ESSAYS ON THE PERFORMING ARTS FROM CURRENCY HOUSE

No. 47
May 2016

CURRENCY HOUSE

Platform Papers Partners

We acknowledge with gratitude our Partners in continuing support of Platform Papers and its mission to widen understanding of performing arts practice and encourage change when it is needed:

Gillian Appleton
Neil Armfield, AO
Anita Luca Belgiorno Nettis Foundation
Jan Bowen
Jane Bridge
Katharine Brisbane, AM
Elizabeth Butcher, AM
Penny Chapman
Robert Connolly
Peter Cooke, OAM
Rowena Cowley and Dr Richard Letts, AM
Michael J. Crouch, AO
Wesley Enoch
Ian Enright
Larry Galbraith
Tony Grierson
Gail Hambly
Wayne Harrison, AM
Campbell Hudson
Professors Bruce King and Denise Bradley, AC
François Kunc
Peter Lee
Peter Lowry, OAM and Carolyn Lowry OAM
Roderick H. McGeoch, AO
David Marr
Harold Mitchell, AC, AO
Joanna Murray-Smith
Helen O'Neil
Martin Portus
Lesley Power
Professor William Purcell
Geoffrey Rush, AC
Dr Merilyn Sleigh
Positive Solutions
Seaborn Broughton Walford Foundation
Sky Foundation
Maisy Stapleton
Augusta Supple
Andrew Upton
Rachel Ward, AM and Bryan Brown, AM
Kim Williams, AM
Professor Di Yerbury, AM

To them and to all subscribers and Friends of Currency House we extend our grateful thanks.

Platform Papers Readers' Forum

Readers' responses to our essays are now posted on our website.

Currency House invites readers to send us considered responses to this or previous Platform Papers in length between 250 and 2000 words. Submissions may be emailed to info@currencyhouse.org.au with a brief biographical note. The Editor welcomes opinion and criticism in the interest of healthy debate but reserves the right to monitor where necessary.

Platform Papers, quarterly essays on the performing arts, are published every February, May, August and November and are available through bookshops, by subscription and on line in paper or electronic version. For details see our website at www.currencyhouse.org.au.

AFTER THE CREATIVE INDUSTRIES: WHY WE NEED A CULTURAL ECONOMY

JUSTIN O'CONNOR

About the Author

JUSTIN O'CONNOR is a cultural activist and an acknowledged global expert on cultural economies. Currently he is Professor of Communications and Cultural Economy at Monash University and visiting chair at Shanghai Jiaotong University. Until 2012 he was Professor in the Creative Industries Faculty, Queensland University of Technology. He has taught performance and cultural industries at the University of Leeds, and between 1995 and 2006 was Director of Manchester Institute for Popular Culture at Manchester Metropolitan University. He has written widely on changing cultures and recently co-edited *The Routledge Companion to the Cultural Industries*. He is completing a book entitled *Cultural Economy in the New Shanghai*, and is working on another, *Global Cultural Economy*. He was a UNESCO expert for the 2005 Convention on the Diversity of Cultural Expressions and convenes the Global Cultural Economy Network

ACKNOWLEDGEMENTS

I'd like to thank my patient and enthusiastic editor Julian Meyrick, who first suggested this Platform Paper, staying to the bitter end snipping my heavy prose into something more presentable. The paper also benefitted from discussions with his team over at the Laboratory Adelaide project at Flinders University. So too thanks to Katharine Brisbane for her unflagging support. Finally, the paper has also been tested on the willing guinea pigs of my Cultural Economy Masters program at Monash University.

1. The Strange Death of Culture and Creativity

Towards the end of 2015 the new Prime Minister Malcolm Turnbull and his minister Christopher Pyne launched a new Innovation and Science agenda at the Commonwealth Scientific and Industrial Research Organisation (CSIRO) in Canberra. After his predecessor Tony Abbott's paeans to coal and cars, and his wholesale trashing of the renewables sector, it was a welcome ray of light. Some pointed out that the breathy eulogies to digital start-ups were made by the same person who oversaw the downgrading of the broadband network on which these would necessarily rely. Others scratched their heads at the $110 million cuts and extensive staff reductions at the very organisation that was supposed to spearhead Australia's exciting, if belated, venture into the twenty-first century. Politics as usual, perhaps. But I was struck by something else. There was hardly any mention of 'creativity'. Innovation would be driven by investment in, and commercialisation of, the so-called STEM disciplines—Science, Technology, Engineering and Mathematics. The 'creative industries' had no place in Turnbull's vision. Indeed, representatives soon claimed that government stances toward copyright and offshore GST-exemption were making things worse for the sector. Further down the line, academics in the Humanities, Arts and Social Science disciplines (HASS), became aware that their contribution to Australia's innovative future had disappeared from view. Again. Two decades after floating the idea that the creative industries were to be the cutting-edge of the new Australian economy—for which a revamped, market-savvy university sector would provide the core skills—the ship of creativity was sinking with all hands.

Two months earlier, in another hemisphere, and visible only to specialists, the United Nations agreed on its updated Sustainable Development Goals (SDGs). Seventeen ambitious aspirations were adopted: for example: End Poverty in all its Forms Everywhere. (Good luck with that). All subject to intense lobbying within and outside the UN. Development is now a multi-trillion-dollar industry, in which huge conglomerates and powerful states seek lucrative contracts to build roads, hospitals, schools, dams and water systems (think China in Africa). None of the seventeen SDGs mention the word 'culture'. An on-line trawl shows many are linked to UN conventions on gender equality, access to education and health, environmental conservation and so on. Yet despite the petitioning by many cultural organisations, including UNESCO itself, the agency behind the UN's

2005 Convention on the 'Protection and Promotion of the Diversity of Cultural Expressions' (the only binding international convention covering the production and distribution of cultural goods and services) culture has no place on the SDGs.

Two random examples, from the navel-gazing of Canberra to the horse-trading of the United Nations. 'So what?' one might say. In this Platform Paper I argue that these two incidents are symptomatic of the low priority of culture in current public policy-making, and that the fate of the creative industries is closely linked to this.

Along with improved health and education outcomes for the general population, culture was one of the central pillars of public policy in the nation-states of Europe and the Americas in the nineteenth century, and of the new nations that emerged across the globe after 1945. All three domains were deemed essential for creating citizens who would form the basis of unified modern nation-states. All three were seen as important public services, provided by the state for the purposes of building collective identity, social cohesion and economic prosperity. Looking at the health and education sectors today we can see how these have altered since 1945. The way they are now financed and administered, what they are expected to provide, and their mode of that provision, have changed radically since we traipsed into state schools and hospitals as a grateful, undifferentiated, passive mass. Nevertheless, health and education remain central to what states are expected to provide, and are clear grounds for the public's electoral verdict upon governments. Can we say the same about culture?

Over the last twenty-five years, how we understand

culture, and what we expect from governments in respect to it, have changed beyond recognition. Some of the reasons for this are the same as health and education: increasing costs; discontent with bureaucracy; demand for control by no-longer-so-passive citizens; the proliferation and dominance of the private sector. But there is little doubt that, far more than in health and education, the fundamental purpose of culture has been questioned across the political spectrum. So much so that it is now extremely difficult to argue for the value of culture to society as a whole, and thus why it should form part of public service provision. Cathy Hunt's recent Platform Paper showed how the destructive and arbitrary actions of Arts Minister George Brandis last year were not an isolated case. Many have pointed to the low priority that *Creative Australia*—Labor's flagship cultural policy launched in 2013—had even within the Rudd-Gillard Government, and the rapidity with which it disappeared into the official underworld.

For anybody actively involved in these debates, the persistent absence of culture from the policy agenda is deeply confusing. Don't features on culture pervade the news media? Aren't dedicated sections tumbling out of the weekend papers and shiny new art galleries popping up in cities across the globe? It was only twenty years ago that culture was felt to have come into its own. Not only had it found a new rationale for government investment, but this rationale had apparently propelled it to the centre of policy-making. In the future, culture and its close derivative 'creativity' were to be as important to the prosperity of the nation as coal and iron in the nineteenth century.

Arguments for the economic benefits of arts

funding—'impacts', 'value-added', 'multipliers'—had been bubbling around since the 1980s. So too had suggestions that employment in the cultural industries (as they were then called) might compensate for jobs disappearing in the rapid de-industrialisation of Europe and North America. The term 'cultural industries', used to describe the mass production and distribution of 'symbolic' goods and services (such as film, television, radio, publishing, recorded music, video games) had already lost much of its pejorative meaning as they were partnered with 'the arts' in a new narrative of cultural and economic transformation. But at the turn of the millennium these arguments hooked up with a new current of economic thinking humming with stories of 'creativity' and 'innovation', especially in the new digital industries coming out of Silicon Valley and New York. The cultural industries were rebadged under the sign of the 'digital' and now set to lead the economic charge. This was the creative industries moment, summarised in typically succinct fashion by John Hartley, whilst rebranding what was the old Queensland Art College as Australia's first Creative Industries Faculty in 2001.

> *The creative industries idea brought creativity from the back door of government, where it had sat for decades holding out the tin cup for arts subsidy—miserable, self-loathing and critical (especially of the hand that fed it), but unwilling to change—around to the front door, where it was introduced to the wealth-creating portfolios, the emergent industry departments, and the enterprise support programmes. Win, Win.*[1]

Few would share the cloudless optimism of this revealing statement now. After a decade at the front door, many in the cultural sector are concerned with what was left at the back. One thing is clear: the first condition of creativity's entrance into government thinking was that it drop its embarrassing links to art and culture. Creativity became tongue-tied as it was forced to speak the language of growth, innovation and financial modelling. Despite endless impact studies and return on investment metrics produced by the big consultancy firms, since 2008 art and culture have been framed as a luxury good superfluous to everyday requirements. Ejected out of the grand entrance, the back door shrank to the size of a porthole. Lose, lose.

In 2006, Stuart Cunningham argued that the 'price to be paid for a creative economy is that the case for arts and culture will become less about their special or exceptional difference, and become diffused into the need for creativity across the economy and society.'[2] A decade on and what that really means is becoming apparent. The abolition of art and culture's 'difference' has resulted not just in their radical diminishment, but in the dwindling energy of the creative economy itself. The diffusion of art and culture across society has been a pouring of water into sand.

*

The rise and fall of the creative industries can be seen as the passing of yet another fad. Buzzwords come and go, art abides. To some extent this is true. It has been an odd paradox of the creative industries era that, at least until recently, investment in major arts institutions has actually gone up. In the UK, New Labour, who invented the whole idea (sort of), significantly increased capital funding for the traditional arts sector.[3] Indeed, many advocates of the creative industries—me included, from time to time—have bemoaned the lack of resources devoted to serious sustained strategies for new start-ups. But more is at stake than the death of another catch-phrase. The rise of the creative industries reflected real socio-economic, cultural and political developments that cannot now be wished away. It articulated real aspirations and opportunities whose disappearance represents a significant loss, not only in themselves but to the larger sector of which they are a part. If the creative industries sink, then they will take art and culture down with them. The spectacle of their demise should not give rise to *schadenfreude*, therefore, with the expectation of a return to normal service in the arts and culture ministries. The collapse of its policy position leaves the field free for the wholesale privatisation of culture, with governments acting as an infrastructure provider and/or consumer protection regulator. So I come not to bury the creative industries, but to hack and reboot them. First, however, we need to look at the origin of the creative industries agenda as whole.

The term 'creative industries' was coined in 1998. It was a last minute neologism used to garnish the UK's Department of Culture, Media and Sport's *Creative Industries Mapping Document.* It provided the then-Minister, Chris Smith, with the confidence to go to the Treasury and ask for more money. 'Creative industries' as an operational concept is highly confused. It has bedevilled conversations in and around the cultural sector for years.

It has generated implausible statistics, as all sorts of activities have been thrown into the creative pot, and a proliferation of port-manteaux terms and confusing synonyms—'cultural-creative', 'creative-digital', 'content', 'copyright', 'experience', 'attention' and, well, 'flat white' economies. Can something be cultural but not creative? Is something creative always cultural? And what about art? Is art different from culture? From being creative? Does digital separate creative from cultural? So what about digital art or live streaming the Metropolitan Opera? Try turning these words into fridge magnets. Move them around, see what sense you come up with.

It is easy to poke fun at the definitional confusions inaugurated by the creative industries. The quick uptake of its verbal coinage has resulted in a semantic quagmire. But its political impact has been very powerful. Governments might not be able to say exactly what it means, but 'creative' seems to open up a more exciting, inspiring vista than the word 'culture', which has taken on an aura of worthiness and preservation, even elitism, by comparison. In the hyper-connected world of spin, perceptions are everything. But the rhetorical shifts around culture and creative were a long time in the making and we should see them as part of an attempt to re-frame social democratic nation-states in the face of a belligerent neo-conservatism and the collapse of the Soviet Union. That's a big jump, so let me briefly lay out this complex backstory.

2. Art into Culture

In the early 1990s a number of United Kingdom Labour politicians, groaning under what was to be eighteen years of Conservative rule, came to Australia to discover what the Hawke-Keating Government had done right. New Labour was to be elected by a landslide at the end of a decade of social democratic resurgence across the English-speaking world. Inspiringly, the visiting British politicians found a thriving democracy seemingly at home in the new globalising world they had begun to embrace. Australia was undertaking new kinds of trade and new kinds of industries in a more sanguine manner than the strife-torn battleground of Thatcher's class war. Just as striking was Australia's ebullient sense of identity, informed by a new multiculturalism, and a rising generation of youth that had grown up in the 1970s and 1980s light years away from the old colonialism, with its cultural cringes and xenophobic fear of outsiders.

*

Keating's influential policy statement *Creative Nation* appeared in 1994, and its catchy title was seized upon by Chris Smith for his own publication—*Creative*

Britain—four years later. *Creative Nation* set out three new themes for Australian cultural policy:

1. to embrace multiculturalism, uncoupling national identity from a bounded sense of 'us and them' in a pluralistic way that is now familiar (though some may regret it);

2. to welcome the popular culture that had transformed Australia's cities and regions since the 1960s, and recognise that much of this was commercially produced and should not be despised because of it. And finally

3. to recognise that culture, in the expanded, all-embracing sense of art, popular culture and effervescent 'ways of life' (including sexual and sub-cultural), was also economically valuable.

The use of the word 'creative' might seem obvious now, but if one looks through arts and cultural policies before 1990, the word hardly rates a mention. 'Culture' had been the crucial term for these documents, as it was in academic scholarship, which over the course of the 1990s had undergone a 'cultural turn', driven along by the ear-studded, jean-wearing doyens of Cultural Studies. The shift from culture to creative was not a terminological whim, but expressed deep shifts in the political tectonics. When an expanded understanding of culture was cast as an economic driver of the creative industries, *Creative Nation* was a pivot point.

First came the shift from art to culture, which in its own way expressed an opening out and democratisation of the arts. The late 1960s and 1970s had brought art down from its pedestal and rooted it in everyday social life. Pierre Bourdieu's *La Distinction*, published in French in 1979, set the academic seal on this, as he took on, with a mix of opaque prose and dense statistics, art's claim to disinterested autonomy.[4] Art was a vehicle enforcing class distinctions. If you felt uncomfortable walking through Greco-Roman porticos, then you were not alone, and hey, it was fine to feel that way. Along with art's reduction in status went the demotion of the figure of the artist as Divine Genius, a figure who fell from the pedestal to the pedal-bin in the blink of a decade, finding an afterlife only on rock music stages. Historians and sociologists agreed that the production of art and culture was not the work of individual talent but a combination of skills, institutions, embedded practices and markets. In 2004 I attended one at the world's largest cultural studies conferences in Hong Kong, at which over six hundred papers were delivered. Flicking through the abstract book, spare time on my hands, I found only two references to 'art'. Raising that absence in the bar later I was met only with guffaws.

In the 1980s culture was everywhere. We were better educated, better off and with free time on our hands. We hated the nine-to-five world (and the harsher, eight-to-four world of the factory) because it was boring. Culture gleamed with the age-old promise of expressive self-realisation previously reserved for the upper classes. Rising unemployment, cushioned by government benefits, proved Ernst Bloch's famous maxim: 'Man shall not live by bread alone, especially when he hasn't got any.'[5] For a new wave of public policy makers, the task was no longer to protect high art from the degradation of the market. The majority of cultural wants—and the new impulses expressed within them—were being satisfied outside state funded institutions. Any truly democratic policy had to acknowledge that fact. Governments committed to cultural democracy and cultural participation had to find a way to work with those outside their own bureaucratic structures and find ways of engagement different from simply providing their 'clients' with 'funding'.

This extension of culture beyond the arts into everyday life, and the need for government cultural agencies to find new ways of dealing with diverse individuals and communities, is a crucial aspect of the sea-changes to which I referred earlier. Ever since the eighteenth century art had been a hallowed world apart, one in which the free play of the imagination was allowed, unencumbered by logic, morality and instrumental rationality. Art was an end in itself precisely because its promise was open-ended. Art was a privileged site whereby the new came into the world. The promethean energies of industry, science and engineering may have been transforming the physical world, but art held the key to the transformation of the soul, and of the association of souls we call society.

Between the 1960s and the 1980s profound social changes also upturned fixed ways of life and identity: different methods of child-rearing, different forms of sexuality, different attitudes to work, and a different relationship with the until-then-taken-for-granted environment in which we lived. When 'natural' relationships melt into air we realise that, as conventions, they can be changed. The word culture began to express a sense of this profound fluidity. It became a symbol for the assertion of a human-centred, democratic, participatory approach to social, economic and political ideas that reflected people's new reality. And it retained its promise of autonomous self-transformation—of individuals and communities—that had previously been exclusively associated with the western art tradition.

Two examples illuminate this. The first is the 'culture and development' movement which from the late 1970s animated anti-colonial anthropologists and development activists. They rejected top-down modernisation as colonial and destructive. They validated local, 'traditional' culture as essential to an equitable, long-term and environmentally non-destructive form of development. They were also anti-capitalist—or at least anti-corporatist—and anti-imperialist. In the late 1980s, many international cultural agencies—UNESCO especially—mobilised around this. Culture—expressed in performance, rituals, art objects and so on—was now as central to development as economics. In 1988 UNESCO declared a World Decade for Culture and Development, in which culture stood for the centrality of locally-rooted ways of life. Fundamental to this was the view that the economy was *not* the be all and end all of development. The economic might even be damaging to local communities, and therefore economic imperatives should be subservient to, or at least mitigated by, cultural considerations.[6]

This new centrality of culture could also be found in the metropolitan heartlands of Europe, North America and

Australia. Here the target was not development but urban planning. New urban social movements rejected top-down planning and the idea of the city as a machine for moving people between work and home. Neighbourhoods and streets, as both Jane Jacobs in Greenwich Village and the *soixante-huitards* in Paris shouted, were where people lived, not just containers for industrial production, financial administration and social welfare. Arguments similar to those of the culture and development activists emerged. Planners needed to speak to and work with people, otherwise more monstrous buildings would be built, more communities trashed. Here again, culture was held up as a way of framing what we value, of how we should live together, and was different from (and larger than) the concept of economic prosperity. It is out of this that we got new urban cultural 'gurus' such as Charles Landry—an early and frequent visitor to Australia—and, further down the line, Richard Florida.

This new understanding of culture was political in a small 'p' way. Inevitably, however, it began to encompass a harder-edged, capital 'P' political strand of thinking concerned not with culture as a way of life, but as a media industry. This looked to the new industrial forms of production, distribution and reception known as the cultural industries: television and radio, print media, film and music. It focused on cultural production by large scale corporate enterprises, and looked to political economy for its analysis. It was concerned not only with media markets and management techniques, but with the social and political context in which they took place, and the space of the 'public sphere', between the state and the economy in which the broad interests of society were debated in a supposedly rational manner. How was it possible, critics asked, to give over responsibility for public culture to a self-interested, ever-diminishing group of multi-national capitalist enterprises?

This is still an important question, and if it is asked less frequently than before, it is because it has been consigned to the *too*-hard basket. During the 1980s, however, three things seemed to relieve the fear of corporate dominance and were used to defend what was happening. First, some argued, people weren't passive dupes and could make up their own minds about the culture they were served, often turning it to their own creative ends. Second, even though such industries were profit-driven enterprises, 'culture' was volatile and unpredictable, driven by ever-changing needs and desires which corporations could neither predict nor control. Profit-driven they might be but these were industries like no other. Finally, it became obvious that—even before the advent of the internet—the production of culture was becoming more decentralised and distributed. Everybody wanted in on culture's act and the availability of cheaper, easy-to-use technology meant that more and more could actually do so. Alongside fears of corporate dominance, then, was a sense that technology might enable unprecedented levels of cultural participation.

In Europe, these strands of thought came together in the popular policies of the French Minister of Culture, Jack Lang, and the Greater London Council's 'cultural industries' program. Two broad aims were clear. First, to regulate the commercial sector in such a way as to foster diversity by working with the small-scale producers.

Rather than adopt an institutional model of state-client subsidy, their focus was now on cooperatives, access to performance and rehearsal space, access to technologies and skills, and on opening up new types of market. The second aim, more emphasised in London than Paris, was to foster their belief that the cultural industries could provide new forms of employment to replace declining industrial jobs. The GLC's cultural industries program grew out of its economic development committee, and after the Council's forced demise in 1986, it was other, mostly Labour, economic development agencies that picked up the idea. Provision of culture was for the public good. It benefited both those who produced it and those who received it: a way that individuals could make a living, and post-industrial cities could look to the future. Win, win indeed.

*

Before looking more closely at the creative industries there is a final strand to be pulled from the bundle, one located in the heady world of economic and industrial geography. Unlike the doyens of neo-classical economics, who believed *homo economicus* made rational decisions based on perfect information in pursuit of benefit maximisation, geographers dealt with real people in a concrete time and place. They could not ignore the obvious fact that cultural industries happened in some places but not in others. Economic activity was not a seamless movement of people and money, it was 'embedded'. Social relations, religious and political beliefs, local networks, skill-sets, market connections, indeed, 'cultures' made all the difference. Cities and regions were 'path dependent', part of a complex historical trajectory which could be altered but not evaded. Wollongong was not going to be Paris, and Sydney was not going to be Hong Kong. To paraphrase Marx, cities might embrace economic development, but not in conditions of their own choosing.

Economic development was not just coloured, facilitated or constrained by the culture in which it was embedded. Economic development increasingly seemed to be *about* culture in two senses. First, modern advanced economies were no longer based on the transformation of raw materials into things to be sold. They dealt in services that enhanced how these things were branded and consumed. Companies could deliver experiences to people without bothering much with things at all. Niche products were bought for how they made you feel, promoted through marketing which spoke to you as an individual with desires and aspirations, around which you could build a 'lifestyle'. To combine these elements across a production chain that stretched between Shenzhen and San Francisco, involved skilled, knowledgeable, people talking to each other. Only cities, and only certain cities could do this—those with dense networks of people drawing on multiple skills able to facilitate and manage connections across complex international supply chains and divisions of labour. All economic activity was embedded in culture. But only the right kind of culture would be useful for the kinds of economic development modern cities required.

As luck would have it, arts and cultural activities *were* the right kind of culture—the visual and performing arts, television and radio, film and music, designer clothes and jewellery, books and magazines. These industries too were found only in certain cities and in certain places in these cities. This was called 'clustering' and by the end of the 1990s discovering a 'cluster' was the local economic development equivalent of striking oil. Clusters offer 'traded interdependencies' - factors that reduce costs through proximity by supporting networks that provide access to key supplies and skilled labour. In addition, there were 'untraded interdependencies'—the circulation of knowhow, and the rules, norms, and institutional practices that define an industrial field. These conditions enable cultural production by bringing together complementary firms and people to provide opportunities for information and resource exchange and exposure to alternative ideas and practices, which propel product innovations and new production processes.

The discovery that the ramshackle collection of bohos, yuppies, arty types, musos, rapacious publishers, exploitative recording companies, hippy street markets, burnt-out clubbers, and very nice people from the ABC was in fact an *agglomeration economy*—nay, a *creative ecosystem*—was very welcome. Finally, validation! Not getting a 'real' job *was the right choice*. Everything they had said about boring people in suits and the idiocy of urban planners was true. It was not only that what cultural producers collectively did was worth something; it was what in the future *everyone* would do. Radicals from the 1960s and 70s popped up in New York penthouses, and featured in densely written books with impressive-sounding titles like '*Economies of Signs and Space*'.[7] These *ad hoc*, instinct driven, slow-growth, micro-firms were no longer economic basket cases scoffed at by smartly dressed business advisors. They were the bleeding edge of the new cultural and informational economy.

3. From Culture to Creative

By the mid-1990s the word 'culture' was working in many different ways for many different people. Culture was to be more participatory, and art no longer overridden by 'experts' but available to everyone. It was also an economy. It provided new employment, generated wealth and contributed to the confidence and energy of a city or a nation. Artists and small businesses, embedded in local cultures, competed but also collaborated. Individual success brought collective returns. Combining technical, creative and interpersonal skills, the cultural sector was part of the new democratic arts infrastructure, plugged into 'the street' with its cafes and shops and popular culture. It was a driver of innovation, a vision of the future. What was not to like?

For the Keating Government and a newly energised Labour Opposition in the UK under Tony Blair, there was no downside. If art was Conservative, culture was left-leaning. Culture was an extension of citizenship, roping in the motley metrosexual constituency along with those better-off in the middle classes who could not stomach the harsh brand of neo-liberalism the Right embraced. Reagan and Thatcher had, improbably, converted Conservatism from a backward-looking to a forward-looking agenda. They were revolutionaries, and they looked more so as the Soviet Union and its Leftist acolytes suddenly turned to stone. But culturally Thatcher and Reagan were still backwards-looking—flags, proper jobs and family values. Now culture could reappear as entrepreneurial but also cool. Keating embraced the hedonic populism *Countdown* promoted. Bill Clinton played sax and Tony Blair the guitar. The cultural industries were giving social democracy back its mojo.

Crucially, in a new age of small states and empowered citizen-consumers the new cultural industries did not demand significant state intervention, simply a recognition that their contribution was strategic, dynamic and popular. It was not about asking for grant money. It was more about investment, training, and different forms of regulation. This was an economic sector bubbling up by its own boot-straps. Governments certainly should support it, but culture was not shipbuilding or steelmaking. The new sector was going to be policy lite.

In order for the cultural industries to morph into the creative industries, two more ingredients were needed. First came the rhetorical rise of the entrepreneur. For most of the twentieth century, the entrepreneur had been a shady figure, a middleman, a door-to-door salesman. In the early 1970s, with the rise of what became known as neo-liberal economics, the entrepreneur returned as the saviour of a capitalism stuck in a cycle of high inflation and low profits. Austrian economist Joseph Schumpeter saw the entrepreneur as key to capitalism's 'creative destruction'. Existing economic models had to be destroyed to make room for the new, and the entrepreneur, working at the margins, breaking the rules, was its driver. As a maverick, iconoclastic figure, running on imagination as much as rational analysis, operating chaotically rather than step by step, the entrepreneur moved closer to the artist's way of working. Creativity emerged as a new force at the heart of the theory of firm, corporate management, and the new innovation economics.

Following closely behind came all things 'digital'. The digital had it all. It came trailing clouds from a Silicon Valley that was (if one ignored the massive state investment, as most tended to do) a pure incarnation of bottom-up originality. For the UK and Australia, having divested themselves of much of their heavy industry, why look to Germany (until 2014 the world's biggest exporter of manufactured goods) when you could have California? California was self-made and hip. It was a perfect example of creativity not only in content but in business approach and in new techniques of production and distribution. The coders, the designers, the business gurus, the content providers—they were all part of the same creative endeavour. The internet was pushing cultural participation further than ever anticipated. Now anybody could produce, and sell it directly to whoever wanted to buy it. No distribution bottlenecks full of rent-seeking gatekeepers. Technology was achieving what public sector regulation had signally failed to do—open up the market for culture to anyone who wanted in. The public sphere was now more open than at any time since the 1920s.

Suddenly the word 'creative' was everywhere. To use it was to align yourself not just with the cool arty types, but also no-collar start-ups, hip entrepreneurs, the coders working 18-hour stints fuelled with Coke and pizza. It provoked a synergy of culture, business and technical skill. Art + technology + enterprise. The days of state regulation of media and culture, and indeed their direct provision, seemed numbered. Creativity, the key resource of the twenty-first century, was to be found in bedsits and on street corners, not science parks and universities. Promoting the creative industries in the 'creative economy' not only aligned nations with the drift of the future, re-inventing industrial policy for a new small-government, carbon-free, consumer-empowered century, it ensured the growth of a young, Left-leaning constituency of voters. Talking to government staffers at this time, and many in the cultural sector itself, it was clear to me that 'creative' was picking up everything 'culture' had had, but with accents of youth, entrepreneurialism, innovation and, inevitably and ubiquitously, digital technology.

Australia was responsible for putting much of this narrative together, not just in *Creative Nation* but also in the cultural policy contributions of some universities. But by the time the digital revolution fully kicked in, the Keating phase was over and the country was settled into the 'comfortable' Howard years, when it was easier to rely on the extraction industries and give tax perks to the middle classes than seek out innovation. In Britain, however, New Labour, with no industry and even less mining, was casting about for something to offset its reliance on financial and business services. The creative industries' agenda was welcomed, if with various degrees of scepticism and lip service. Here was an invitation to the policy table (via the grand entrance) for the cultural sector.

The creative industries marked a highly successful branding exercise for the UK. 'Cool Britannia' was rhetorical flummery certainly, but it recognised the high levels of commercial and professional experience that could be gathered to promote the United Kingdom as a new kind of economy. It was also phenomenally successful in East Asia, in the former Eastern European countries and in some western European countries who were thinking more about the economic dimension of culture in the age of innovation. This recognition of culture that the creative industries seemed to herald gave confidence to a loose policy constituency that for decades had been pushing for culture's integration into planning and development.

One wicked question, however, persistently resurfaced. What exactly *were* the creative industries?

*

To measure the cultural sector in his meetings with Treasury bean counters, one of the most powerful weapons Chris Smith wielded was a set of figures on the cultural sector. It employed, he claimed, 1.3 million people and contributed £112.5 billion to the economy.[8] During the 1990s the measurement of cultural sector employment and GDP had become more sophisticated, and this accelerated with the rise of the creative economy. The creative industries were the cultural industries (film, TV, radio, print, music, design, fashion, visual and performing arts) with software added. Culture + digital. A problem was this 'software' segment made up 40%+ of the employment figure, and continued to do so in subsequent statistical exercises. Calling it 'creative industries' then not only gave it a digital patina, it claimed the digital sector for itself. Doubling the size of its constituency by adding its fastest growing sub-sector was part of creativity's attraction. At the time only the statistical policy geeks (that'll be me) were concerned that we were adding database developers for financial services to the cultural sector.

Doubts about the idea of the creativity industries become pronounced when the *Mapping Document* is examined more closely:

> *Those industries which have their origin in individual creativity, skill and talent and which have a potential for wealth and job creation through the generation and exploitation of intellectual property.*[9]

Here 'creative' is used as a general capacity for innovation and imagination. It is 'making money from ideas', though not all those ideas—a patent for an industrial process, for example, or a sub-prime mortgage algorithm—could be described as cultural.[10] Richard Florida, an economic geographer who stumbled into a career as one of the world's best-paid academic consultants, defined his 'creative class' precisely in this way. He included scientists and other professionals who collectively made up around 40 per cent of the workforce. Potentially it included everyone apart from blue-collar workers who were consigned, along with the towns they lived in, to the historical dustbin.[11]

More recently, we've had the 'flat-white' economy which includes 'media, marketing, IT, communications, finance and cultural industries.'[12] It should be clear by now that precision of definitions is *so* twentieth century.

This problem has never gone away. I teach masters students from all over the world, who all ask me the same question—what does the 'creative industries' mean? They never ask what the arts are (though they might ask what art is) or what the cultural industries are—though they might be confused as to whether either are creative. It is particularly fraught in East Asia, where creative industries can include business consulting, bio-tech, advanced manufacturing, R&D services and other ideas-driven sectors. In fact, some East Asian countries in a *reductio ad absurdum* deliberately exclude 'culture', which is seen as something else again!

It was never quite like this in the UK or in Australia, where the creative industries idea was heavily promoted by Queensland University of Technology. But fundamental questions remained. Is 'cultural' a sub-sector of 'creative', or are they two sectors? Does 'creative industry' simply mean that art and culture are 'applied' to things, or to 'the digital', or to the 'commercial'. Is all of design a creative industry, or just the bits that were about surface appearance and marketing? Should the needs of software engineers be addressed in the same way as arts practitioners? In 2008, the UK's Department of Culture Media and Sport (DCMS) decided to drop software from its sector statistics. Digital technologies had enormous impact on the cultural sector but to call software development in the financial sector 'creative' was a category error. Digital skills and platforms were crucial for culture, but they were crucial also in health and education. This did not make those who developed them part of the sector.

This is not a bun fight amongst stats geeks but fundamental to building the modus operandi of a creative industries strategy. Whom do you actually target, on what basis and through what means? If we were unclear what 'creative' includes, then policy became a matter of loose interpretation, with policy approaches reflecting the idiosyncrasies of whatever definition we decided to use. But there is a deeper issue. In the shift from culture to creative we lost not only definitional clarity but our understanding of the very value of culture. Culture refers to a way of life, a stock of knowledge and symbolic meanings, and a set of artifacts, practices and processes that express and speak to this. Creativity, though exemplifying certain qualities derived from our *use* of culture, can too easily be translated into no more than a production input.

*

This is exactly what happened. After 2007, to convince governments the creative industries were a serious economic force, agencies like the Centre of Excellence for the Creative Industries and Innovation (CCI) in Australia, and NESTA in the UK, sought new ways to identify and measure 'creative inputs'. Rather than counting culture + digital + design + marketing, they counted everyone engaged in creative occupations wherever they were. An artist working in a school or hospital. A pianist on a cruise ship. This was fine and had been done in the 1990s by both the Australia Council and the Arts Council in the UK. What was new was that, CCI and NESTA between them redefined what this creative input was.[13]

The final leap. Creativity now became: 'the application of creative talent to commercial ends' and a creative occupation was identified as

> *a role within the creative process that brings cognitive skills to bear about differentiation to yield either novel or significantly enhanced products whose final form is not fully specified in advance.*

The first thing to say is that surgeons, teachers, and business consultants all do this. So why are they not being counted? Though the official statistical computations may be fancier, the definitional is simply being kicked down the road. The second is to say that arts and cultural industries had always been classified—and indeed judged—in terms of their *outputs*. 'This is cultural (even if bad). This is not (even if good).' With creativity treated as an input, it does not matter what the quality of the output is or its ultimate purpose. If it adds value, it's creative.

This is the heart of the quagmire. The divine spark passed on to mankind through Adam's finger is reduced to a non-repetitive value-adding input to a commercial product. Those who argued for the cultural and creative industries at the turn of the millennium did so convinced the new combination of culture + economy was about more than profit maximisation. They thought they had proved that culture—its networks and institutions, passions and desires, communities and ecosystems—could not be reduced to simply money. But they were wrong. The desire to prove that creativity was economically valuable succeeded at the cost of making culture disappear.

4. Life in the Creative Industries

During the Rudd-Gillard era, the creative industries returned to Australia less as an industrial than an educational agenda. Australia, basking in a commodities boom, did not have to trouble itself at a federal level with creative industries policies. Queensland Labor, re-inventing itself after the Joh years, was the nearest Australia got to New Labour, with a generation of young leaders seeking a future that was not about unions and jobs protection. On their doorstep was a university keen to redefine what culture and creative education might be. After the Dawkins reforms of higher education in the 1980s, which introduced market principles to the education sector, the Humanities sought new justifications for their existence. The arts especially, staring economic unviability in the face, took strongly to the notion of 'creativity' as a response to life in a volatile, changing world. QUT acted as a prime mover with a re-designation of its arts school as a Creative Industries Faculty. Others soon followed.

This also happened in the UK and across Europe. In

Australia however, its provenance in a university dominated by creative industry proselytizers gave it an edge it lacked elsewhere. Putting the creative arts at the centre of the new economy was one thing. Declaring art was dead, with culture to follow, was another. Welcoming commercial cultural production as legitimate was one thing. Saying only the commercial was truly democratic was another. The creative industries polarised the cultural constituency that in the UK trundled along under a new flag of convenience. In Australia, there were no fellow-travellers, only true believers.

It was particularly in the area of creative labour that the creative industries made its mark. The new creative workforce, entrepreneurial, at home with volatility and risk, was going to redefine Arts and Humanities Departments. It is in part because of this emphasis that so much of creative industries research has focused on employment statistics: the shock troops used to demonstrate the phenomenal growth of the sector and the continued relevance of those supplying labour to it.

Elsewhere in the economy, however, other things were happening. As the decade rolled on, the vision of a creative industries sector as a process of self-expression *and* a way of making a living, began to peel and fade. Entry into the cultural sector actually became harder. Those in it worked long, unsocial hours. They did free labour, they received low pay. Secure work replaced by the 'gig' economy. Towards the end of the decade, policy-makers began to encounter terms like 'self-exploitation' and 'precariat',[14] and the image of the creative entrepreneur began to harden. Workers were told they had to be creative and entrepreneurial *or else.*

The shine came off creative labour and even the digital revolution began to look jaded. A new law of internet-based economies had emerged. Let a thousand flowers bloom ... but the biggest and brightest will cannibalise the rest. No longer on a local but a global scale. Facebook, Apple, Google, Amazon now bestride the world in ways of which Time Warner and EMI only dreamt. Anyone can sell to anyone—but don't give up your day job because unless you sell through [insert your internet aggregator here] you'll be another loser in a long loser's tale.

There was an unlooked-for return of the corporate Dinosaurs. Seemingly on their way to extinction as 'disruptive technologies' eviscerated their business models, they came back bigger and stronger than ever. Film companies did deals with digital distribution platforms, as did the music companies, once they got over the shock. Publishers did not like Amazon, but the major players could find a way around it. The fact that the new internet companies now displayed a winner-take-all character made them more manageable from the corporatist point of view. They were people with whom you could do business. Indeed, both old and new companies were increasingly part of another transformation sweeping the world—financialisation. Increasingly, capital moved into actual industries only if it could convert their business into financial assets. In response to the disruptions of the late 1990s, and later, the Global Financial Crisis, the big cultural corporations restructured themselves around their assets—tradable intangibles protected by internationally enforced copyright laws. Diversifying, merging, divesting and acquiring, they sought big and rapid returns to keep their asset value high.

Financial assets are best managed if distribution is secure, guaranteed by a method tried and true—monopoly (or duopoly for the sake of a quiet life). Those in control are thus in a position of dominance. The arrival of digitalisation undermined the traditional ways of monetising content. It took some time, but through links to the new internet platforms run by the old telecoms, along with new methods for making home viewing chargeable, large-scale content providers began once again to dominate the market.

In retrospect, the vision of a new creative economy in which anyone could sell to anyone, and creative labour was self-fulfilling and abundantly rewarded, was as far from the truth as it was possible to get. Monopoly control now happens on a global scale. It favours those companies who do not actually produce its aggregated content and so have little interest in cultural production. Not only have the Government's policy levers corroded but so too have the grounds for political intervention. While our publicly funded arts sector remains committed to openness, participation, and engaging the diverse experience of its audiences, the large cultural corporations have become more commercial, more centralised and less committed to anything other than the maximisation of profit. States have little inclination and less power to make change. This is the reality the term 'creative industries' masks.

5. Where we are now: inflated rhetoric and policy confusion

In severely abbreviated form, and with due apology for the resulting simplification, what I have been describing is the fall of the creative industries. The creative industries idea articulated a range of expectations about culture and its economic and social impact. It did not begin as a reduction of culture to economics but as an attempt to combine culture and the economy in a way that would bring growth and increased participation—a creative *and* a prosperous society. It outlined an attractive and do-able policy agenda (no multi-billion dollar facilities needed!) which transformed the cultural sector into an object of government innovation policy. It captured the zeitgeist, and in a new age of Apple, Netflix and Sotheby's International recognised that the well-worn defensive responses from the traditional arts community were no longer viable. Creative industries brought together an economic vision—making money through ideas in a weightless digital economy—and a conception of individual and collective creativity that went right back to Frederick Schiller in the eighteenth century. Schiller was the first to argue that the sensual and the rational combined in the creative play of art, to create a form of knowledge quite different from ethical or logical reasoning. The fuel core of creativity lying at the heart of the western art tradition would now drive a collective participation in commercial innovation.

The dream of such an alliance has not entirely gone away. It is there as a kind of dull default, a nod to the youthful world of digital start-ups sitting uneasily with the remnants of previous cultural policy. The arts—mostly the flagships, but sometimes the flotilla as well—do all the principled work on public funding. The cultural industries do capitalism, red in tooth and claw. The arts bear the residual idealism of earlier cultural policy (on an ever-dwindling budget) while the creative industries do the economic heavy lifting required today. To mangle Theodor Adorno, both are torn halves of an integral whole to which they do not add up. The destructive consequences of art becoming yet again the preserve of a monied class (however radically chic) while the rest of culture is left to the predations of big capital, are barely discerned. The demise of the newspapers and the critical journalism they supported, and the relaxation of media ownership, now seen as relevant only to 'old technology', speaks of the radical failure of cultural policy-making in Australia. It is not alone. The fetishism of technological change, combined with a belief that the market is king, has been a catastrophe for a global creative industries agenda that saw itself as master signifier of the future. The robots, in the form of increasingly computerised services, financial algorithms, and government metrics, are winning.

Briefly, I want to take a closer look at the economic agenda around the creative industries. Two things strike me as odd. First, while seeking to expand the definition of creativity to boost its economic impact, creative industry proselytisers actually succeeded in *narrowing* it to a specialist sector. Second, despite the open reception given to its 'easy sell' message, Australian governments have done almost nothing to support it. Which on the face of it confirms what sceptics say: that presenting culture as commercial simply allows governments to see it as a self-sustaining activity. It is a bit more complex than that, however.

I argued above that extending creativity to all sorts of activities in an attempt to 'steal' employment figures for the sector has led to a conceptual confusion and an erosion of creativity's specificity. I have discussed its definitional problems at length elsewhere, and will only summarise them here.[15] The European Union's recent Green Paper makes a distinction between cultural and creative industries. The former includes the visual and performing arts, television and radio, film, recorded music, print and publishing. Like other documents before it, it emphasises the centrality of symbolic or aesthetic value to cultural products. The creative industries are 'applied' cultural products—fashion, design, architecture, marketing and so on—where the symbolic, aesthetic or cultural aspect is only one part of the end result. I believe this is a false distinction that sneaks in all sorts of old, unwelcome hierarchies. The EU introduced it in order to apply cultural policy standards to the former and commercial standards to the latter. In practice, it leads to an arts versus cultural industries divide.[16] There is, however, a perfectly workable

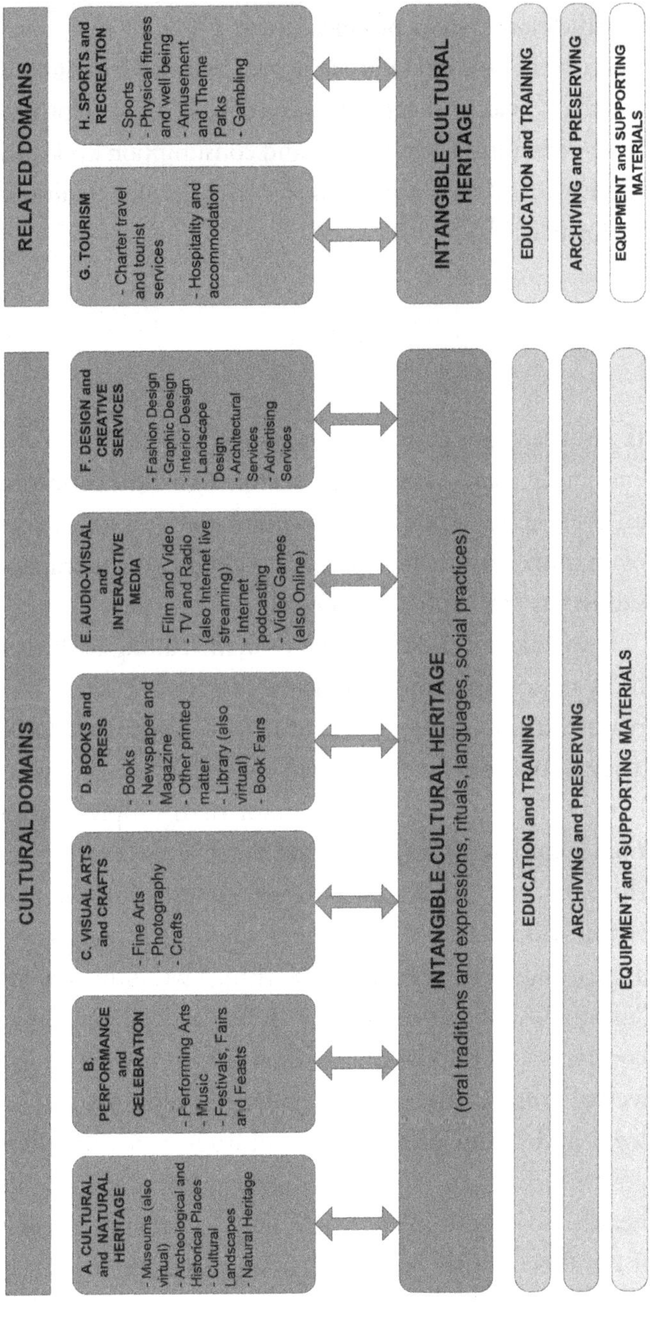
CULTURAL DOMAINS
A. CULTURAL and NATURAL HERITAGE
- Museums (also virtual)
- Archeological and Historical Places
- Cultural Landscapes
- Natural Heritage
B. PERFORMANCE and CELEBRATION
- Performing Arts
- Music
- Festivals, Fairs and Feasts
C. VISUAL ARTS and CRAFTS
- Fine Arts
- Photography
- Crafts
D. BOOKS and PRESS
- Books
- Newspaper and Magazine
- Other printed matter
- Library (also virtual)
- Book Fairs
E. AUDIO-VISUAL and INTERACTIVE MEDIA
- Film and Video
- TV and Radio (also Internet live streaming)
- Internet podcasting
- Video Games (also Online)
F. DESIGN and CREATIVE SERVICES
- Fashion Design
- Graphic Design
- Interior Design
- Landscape Design
- Architectural Services
- Advertising Services
INTANGIBLE CULTURAL HERITAGE
(oral traditions and expressions, rituals, languages, social practices)
EDUCATION and TRAINING
ARCHIVING and PRESERVING
EQUIPMENT and SUPPORTING MATERIALS
RELATED DOMAINS
G. TOURISM
- Charter travel and tourist services
- Hospitality and accommodation
H. SPORTS and RECREATION
- Sports
- Physical fitness and well being
- Amusement and Theme Parks
- Gambling
INTANGIBLE CULTURAL HERITAGE
EDUCATION and TRAINING
ARCHIVING and PRESERVING
EQUIPMENT and SUPPORTING MATERIALS

classification system produced by UNESCO that covers the arts, the cultural industries, and the broader design and creative services. Taken together they are seen as forming the entire cultural production and consumption cycle. The UNESCO schema also allows for heritage and traditional performance.[17]

*

If we accept this classification system one thing becomes eminently clear—it is a vast sector with connections to an even larger one of public education, and to all sorts of manufacturing (computers) and mineral extraction industries (no copper, no digital).

If we take all these cultural domains, along with their links to tourism and recreation, we have a sector that makes up around 20 per cent of advanced countries' GDP. They also sweep in things that make a lot of life worth living. There is more to this sector than simply innovation: it embraces celebrating and socialising, learning and thinking, relaxation and catharsis, imagination and play, self-development and communal bonding, that are key to a meaningful future. All those things we somehow call 'culture'. At the same time, it is also an economy, with contracts and purchases, wages and commissions, intellectual property and grants, regulations and technologies, legal and financial services, buildings and caretakers, governments and entrepreneurs. It is an economy, like health and education are economies, but economic benefit it not their primary or exclusive purpose.

Perhaps because its tradition of supporting small-scale cultural producers was seen as a progressive agenda—a bottom-up challenge to authority—the creative industries had always had an emphasis on production. It had also assumed the market was the most efficient allocation mechanism and now, in the age of the internet, who needs state provision? So 'creative industries' focused on redefining government funding as *investment*. But it was never clear what governments were expected to do. The primary target was support for small businesses, through workspace provision, access to finance, business training, trade fairs, prizes, competitions and festivals. This was predicated on a newly-held belief that having an industry policy was a thing of the past. Governments do not 'pick winners', the market does. Ignoring the evidence to the contrary, both in the expanding Asian economies and the massive subsidies to its own mining sector, Australian governments gave up on industry policy. The creative industries became simply about training, a bit of pump-priming, and that was that.

*

I have been struck how even though the arts sector fears the creative industries, support has flowed—in an admittedly under-funded sector—to the arts rather than creative industry agencies. This is understandable. The arts are real and tangible, the creative industries uncertain and dispersed. Governments do not want to commit money to a sector with no real referent, lobby group or 'champion'.

So the creative industries have become *the opposite* of an innovation-driven vision of the future. They have become glamorous fluff for governments to show they are doing something for 'creativity'. A film festival and a fashion show work very well in this respect. Other things—actually making films or dealing with the absence of a domestic textile industry—have proved more difficult to address.

When we look at creative industry policy initiatives in Australia it is thin on the ground. Queensland has been closely linked to it, but the main outcomes appear to be a new QUT campus at Kelvin Grove and an academic research centre. Film and fashion have received intermittent support, as have design and the music industry, mainly through the re-designation of Fortitude Valley, (now subject to curfew). Of federal initiatives, Enterprise Connect (abolished by the Abbott Government) has been the most significant. The Rudd Government extended this support scheme to the creative sector. It did a lot of good work—in Victoria especially—but its threshold was set too high for most creative firms ($1 million turnover). It ended up focusing mainly on design businesses. As with most creative industries strategies the world over, the aim was high growth. If you claim to be an economic sector, then get employing, and if you can't, then compensate with a bit of high profile glamour. Recently Arts Victoria renamed itself Creative Victoria. There was no new money, simply a bringing in of commercial ('creative') activities—film, games, design—into the Arts portfolio, and in turn submerging the new agency in an immense economic development pool. No new thinking underpinned this shift—just a vague sense that as creativity is economic it should benefit from going into an economic portfolio. Those with knowledge of how this has panned out elsewhere in the world won't be getting their hopes up.

The latest Creative Victoria strategic plan makes interesting reading.[18] It displays a more nuanced understanding of the needs of a diverse sector and flags culture's connections to a social and the urban context. It is also clear that the arts—metropolitan and regional—are its main business. The document avoids any attempt at a grand narrative. The default is a publicly funded core surrounded by an ecosystem of small business which is to be given support as a form of 'creative' or 'social' enterprise. The assumption is that innovative and 'sustainable' business models can be encouraged, with some 'access to market' initiatives (databases of local musicians, for example), in a classic 'supply-side' model that was outlined by the DCMS nearly two decades ago. But just as the plan avoids the difficult question of 'why', it avoids the analysis of 'how'. Victoria's cultural ecosystem is operating in an age of corporate giants, secretive trade agreements, the symbiosis of real estate and planning, and powerful telecom lobbies. How in practice will it work? Creative Victoria seems stuck for an answer. It is not the fault of the cultural agency. It has a remit for the arts sector. The addition of the cultural (or confusingly, the creative) industries is simply beyond its capacity to manage.

A contrast can be drawn with China, or Korea, or Singapore, or even Germany. These countries have a much clearer idea of what they are doing. Whatever terms and definitions are deployed, they are backed with serious research and development money. Do you want a film industry? Then build production and distribution facilities, or send a State Owned Enterprise to buy them in the US. Or give everybody fast cheap broadband. Or provide music education for everyone in schools.

To understand the conditions within which the cultural sector operates is a difficult task. Thus far, research has tended to be economic, 'mapping' employment and value-added as a way of justifying increased funding. But understanding the landscape in which cultural industries now operate involves long-term investigation and commitment. City councils no longer have this capacity. The kind of iterative exchanges, trust-building and relationship-building between cities and academics are also hard to come by. Examples exist elsewhere, of course, in the UK and Europe. In Australia, however, collaboration has been patchy and self-serving on both sides. Levels of research investment by government and the private sector are way down the OECD league tables, as is our spending on higher education and on arts and culture itself. 'Only in Australia could we announce something called a "Global Innovation Strategy" and assign only $7 million a year for it,' Mark Dodgson of the University of Queensland's Business School said recently. And a contributor to *The Monthly* observed:

> *If the Government limits its definition of innovation simply to a small band of feckless free-marketeers who will be largely the only ones to benefit from it, what hope is there for the society it governs?*[19]

We might add, what hope for a meaningful cultural policy either?

6. The Collapse of Public Value in Public Policy

The problems run deep. For example, the focus on developing cultural firms has been entirely 'supply side'. It has encouraged firms to develop new 'business models' and become more entrepreneurial, then turned them over to the market. This is like raising pedigree chickens and then setting them loose down a foxhole. The focus on 'business modelling' ignores the reality of an economy dominated by a few major players that could eat a city council creative industries office for breakfast. Strategies talk constantly of the market but studiously avoid its realities. I am suggesting, therefore, not a retreat from the market but a rigorous and open-eyed engagement with the actually existing market and the political-regulatory arrangements that underpin it.

One of the chief weaknesses of Australian cultural policy-making has been the separation of cultural policy from that of media and broadcasting. One of the things Tony Blair got right was the creation of a Department of Culture, Media and

Sport. In Australia, these portfolios are split across ministers and departments, with art and culture regularly mixed in with responsibility for sewerage, pig rearing and putting fiberglass in lofts. Two acronyms sum it up, NBN and ABC.

It would take a very self-interested, short-term, politically embittered government to think that catching up with East Asia and Estonia in internet infrastructure was a bad thing. Yet a country with almost the highest per capital income on the globe has created a fibre-optic network stuck into people's homes with the engineering equivalent of Blu-Tack. And it is still over time and over cost! The NBN represents not just a piece of important infrastructure but a chance to discuss what media is, and where it belongs in a modern civilised democracy that can no longer rely on making cheap goods and digging rocks out of the ground. The implosion of Rudd's climate change-program before the lobbying of the mining industry was a major catastrophe. Discarding the chance to build a quality NBN under pressure from the telecoms and media moguls is another. That one failure alone outweighs all the mapping documents and film festivals launched by the creative industries agenda.

Like the NBN, the ABC should be at the centre of any creative industries strategy. Like the UK's BBC it fits awkwardly with that agenda. Both are big corporations and are publicly funded. Both are commercially successful and immensely popular. And yet the fact that they are government supported has been seen not as a public good but as a distortion of the market, a crowding out of the private sector. The ABC is a large entity that clearly has to be financially accountable. But it also has public service remits. It is a microcosm of the sorts of challenges cultural policy should be addressing on a broader scale. It is essential to many local creative ecosystems, and yet has to deal with global players. It must source content and produce its own within a complex system of collaboration, commissioning and purchase. It has responsibilities for the training and development of the sector, for ethical practice and sustainability, for investing in the future, and for gender, ethnic and social equity. And this does not exhaust its remit.

Unlike most creative industries enterprises, the ABC has a responsibility for consumption. The ABC is constrained by a need for audiences, but cannot focus solely on viewer numbers. It has to represent and give space to the opinions, tastes and experiences of a diverse Australian nation. It is part of the world of news journalism, but also the world of cultural affect and emotion, commonality and difference. It must make daily judgements about what should be presented in the public interest. What this may be is a complex question. Some argue there is no such thing in the age of infinite consumer choice. But that is quite wrong. What that public interest is, and how it can be secured, is *exactly* what a cultural policy conversation should be addressing. It should not be hived off, as it increasingly is, to media industry experts and telecom pundits.

At the time of writing, the Federal Arts portfolio has been linked to that of Communications. One of Minister Fifield's first acts, on appointment in 2015, was to relax Paul Keating's media ownership laws restricting single ownership of radio, television and the press. While this was proposed on the ground of a changing market, it was motivated by a combination of technological determinism and corporate interest. Only a residual concern for regional Australia has managed to keep some sort of public interest argument in the frame.

*

Which brings us full circle, to industry policy. An industry policy for culture cannot just be about sales or profit. Like education and health it *does* involve sales and profits, but it would be madness to see these as the basis of those policies. Yet this is what is happening with culture. Our media policy ('culture' having been removed from it entirely, it seems) is now about carriers and IP protection, subscriptions and bandwidths. The question about where the public interest lies is simply not being asked. A recent UK strategic plan contains nothing about the public interest, just the usual blather about the efficiency of technologically-enabled access to ever proliferating points of purchase.[20]

I am not arguing that the economic dimension of the cultural sector is irrelevant, that the measuring of its impacts and metrics is not useful, or that these cannot be part of an overall justification for cultural policy. It is important to know that, based on ABS statistics, the cultural sector employs as many people as construction and more than farming. It is important to know that as an English-speaking country next door to the world's largest emerging market, Australia remains a net importer of cultural goods and services, trading at a level below the Netherlands and other smaller countries.[21] What has never been convincingly shown, because the creative industries agenda has not been interested, is the *value* of the arts, culture, recreation, tourism sector both in itself and as an input into other areas.

This would not, unlike Douglas Adams' meaning of life, appear as a number. It is surely by now widely understood that coming up with a stand-alone figure expressing the worth of this or that cultural activity gets you nowhere. If the Government is on your side, you're fine. If it is not, then no amount of statistics will make them care. Sitting next to Cate Blanchett at an award dinner will do more than any exhaustively computed algorithm. We need numbers, they tell us things. But we have to know *what* they are telling us and *then* make judgements. Quantitative results require a comprehensive understanding of the sector as a broad set of activities involved in the production, distribution and consumption of culture. The resulting strategy would then be not just about how to 'grow' the sector but give a sense of what 'growth' might mean. What kind of growth? 'And to what end? The creative industries' concern with inserting creativity into the 'social innovation system' has not only narrowed culture's use but obscured its economic role as complex services sector with links to other sectors.

Compared with health and education, culture is dispersed and ambiguous. In some aspects it is a core function of the state. In others, a matter of personal consumption choice. Some of its sub-sectors are growing more quickly than others. Some have a direct impact on product and service development. Some are provided for directly out of taxation. Others are market driven. Some are exportable, some less so. Some are able to increase their productivity by capital substitution. Others are relatively impervious to this.

The growth of cultural consumption (education, wealth, leisure time) and the importance of cultural services to other manufacturing and producer service sectors have caused a legitimation crisis in cultural policy. There are real debates about whether, how, and how far, the public should directly subsidise culture. But also whether, how and how far the state should be concerned with the parameters, quality, and level of provision of culture or media. This makes for difficult policy-making. The rationale for arts funding has been reduced to a bare stump of 'excellence' and the remit of the ABC to the politicians' cry for 'balance'. However, the real problem lies in the erosion of a shared language of public value, one that has had a more direct impact on culture than on almost anything else.

Its origins lie in the change in political legitimation and techniques of rule brought about by neo-liberalism. The ideological assertion of the free market as a central tenet of modern government, propounded by Reagan and Thatcher in the 1980s, was more than just a 'rolling back' of the state from the economy. It was a profound shift in political values—'private better than public, individual better than society, rich more attractive than poor, a symbiosis of big money and small politics'[22]—that turned out to be a shift in how we measure value itself. Friedrich Hayek, the father of neo-liberalism, never intended free market principles to be applied to other aspects of society.

It was economists like Milton Friedman of the so-called Chicago School, who suggested that all aspects of public policy be judged on the basis of economic efficiency, and, indeed, managed as if they were quasi-markets. Public administration was restructured around targets that introduced competition (and elimination) into its operations. Health and education developed internal markets, league tables and targets to mimic competition in the 'real world'—and ensure the victory of the most 'efficient'.

How was culture to remain immune from this? The arts got attendance and participation targets, and the media got internal markets and public private partnerships. Both got 'value-for-money' and 'return on investment'. Neo-liberalism has been called the revenge of economics on a politics that had interfered with the market for too long. Like the sorcerer's apprentice's broom, the principles of economic efficiency, built on the satisfaction of individual 'wants', has multiplied and eaten into the central functions of the state itself. Neo-liberalism is a kind of auto-immune disease. Many of the core public justifications of the modern state—even defence, increasingly—are now almost impossible to describe *outside* economic value. The proliferation of using economic measures to nail down in terms of a metric the 'real cost'—early school leaving, work days lost by depression, the value of a university degree or investment in a museum—have made it hard to talk of value in a way that does not sound soft, wishy-washy, and so very chattering class.

7. Rediscovering the Value of Culture

The consequence of all this on our national politics is now clear. It has made any political goal other than serving the economy hard to argue. Just as old-style conservatism made a fatal alliance with Fascism in the 1930s, modern liberals have redefined liberty in such exclusively market-efficiency terms it is impossible for them to declare for wider public values. Democracy, liberty, the rule of law—their main justification now primarily serves simply to underpin the free market. This is what separates the two Malcolms, Fraser and Turnbull. It is fast leading to a political nihilism in which national cohesion is secured by fear, backed up by unprecedented levels of surveillance, control and coercion, rather than by any awareness of the individual's stake in a broad collective enterprise.

The values of culture were always, since the end of the 19th century, about something more than, and different from, the instrumental world of economics and administration and concerned with a fundamental question: how is Australia possible? What binds us together as a society and a nation? The question could be answered in different ways, of course: conservative, revolutionary, social-democratic or liberal-democratic. But the point was that culture articulated it in a space distinct from economics and in a way that directly informed public policy-making. We were citizens and patriots, rebellious and dutiful by turns. Cultural policy was an attempt to create institutions that would reflect, create or mould these roles into a functioning unity. Culture was also about self-development, it asked questions about authentic individual experience and the infrastructure required for its extension. Neo-liberalism has removed the need for all this. Culture as self-development—when not dismissed as code for elitism—now best secured by cost-effective market mechanisms of distribution, choice and purchase, and we are all bound together by our aggregated acts of purchase.

Neo-liberalism, as an active reforming agenda may now be moribund but at present there is not much to replace it, and interregnums breed monsters. The various constituencies that make up the cultural sector face a Herculean task. They have spent a decade trying to show they are useful to governments who increasingly look elsewhere to deliver what culture once did. Now they must re-articulate the public value of culture in a new, inhospitable landscape as a matter of urgency. Art and culture are under immense threat. I am not thinking only about those sustained by public subsidy but about the fate of culture itself. Our system of collective and individual meaning-making has been given over to a market-machine for the capture of 'profit without production', whose dominating logic is financialisation and the battery of digitised metrics that goes along with it.[23] We are engaged in an immense experiment to see if the act of monetary exchange can found not just a dynamic economy but the very basis of social existence and individual fulfillment. It is as crazy as Pol Pot's Year Zero or Mao's Cultural Revolution.

We need a new articulation of the social cohesion and individual fulfilment for which culture once so obviously stood. In this we cannot retreat into a defence of art as ineffable and its payment a matter for somebody else's accountant. We have to recognise that it is an economy but we cannot let the value of that economy be defined exclusively by economists. We could be inspired by how feminist economists discovered vast reservoirs of domestic labour that never found their way into official statistics. Or environmental economists who have shown how disastrous have been the 'externalities' that fail to show up on company balance sheets. Or developmental economists who have found immeasurable value in the local cultures that mainstream development has rejected. Each of these have resisted the abstract logic of econometrics and sought to subject our individual and collective economic actions to social, ethical and political values. The various practices of art and culture give texture and shape to our individual and collective lives, and how we relate to the world around us. We cannot allow these to be overruled by abstract machines of market efficiency and return on investment. Finding this new language of cultural value in an age when culture does have immense economic value is going to be the key challenge of the next two decades.

For example, the current (2016) debate around a potential merger between the ABC and SBS is being conducted in an impoverished language of shared infrastructure and revenue collection. Clearly, some bold re-assertion of public value is required here. At the same time, as Colin Griffith has argued, the new ecology offers the opportunity to re-think the ABC so public value is secured as much by the way it intersects with the production capacities of the wider cultural landscape as in the quality of its content:

> *A merger with SBS is not the route to media diversity and the future of the ABC. The real challenge for the ABC is how to reinvent itself to be become a more open and collaborative organisation in this new media landscape whilst maintaining its independence and trusted role with the Australian community. The ABC should be not just a glorious but isolated example of programming excellence but also a vital contributor to a wider ecosystem of innovation and creative endeavour in Australia.*[24]

Understanding the changing economic configuration of the vastly complex ecosystem of public media institutions and re-purposing this for the delivery of a number of public policy outcomes is absolutely crucial. It demands a re-think of public media organisations. They should not be seen as a rump provision for the things the market doesn't want (like regional content, investigative journalism and the arts) but as part of a restructuring of the market to provide outcomes that we value.

Cathy Hunt called strongly for a re-thinking of the way we publicly support our arts—from the flagships to the flotilla—moving away from the rigidities of a funding system established for another place, another time. George Brandis' cuts to the Australia Council—not restored by the current Government—have not only trashed the collective business plans of hundreds of arts organisations, but nipped in the bud a new conversation about how government funds can be used to multiply public value outcomes. Understanding the arts ecology allows us to develop a whole variety of new arrangements, tools and protocols based not on cost-cutting and off-loading subsidy onto corporate sponsorship but on securing innovation, diversity and sustainable incomes as part of a healthy cultural economy.

Which brings us to one of the most dysfunctional aspects of the cultural economy: real estate. It is a fact universally acknowledged that those who are the net gainers from culture-led regeneration, creative industries, creative place-making, creative clustering and the like are property developers. City councils in turn, despite all their creative rhetoric, look to the tax revenue and rental increase as the absolute index of urban success. The consequences of this for cultural policy have been enormous. Just outside Hobart, by sheer chance, a local-lad-made-millionaire plonked down one of the most exciting new museums in the southern hemisphere. MONA was a surprise gift, one so large and unexpected that it took the city and state some time to fully get their heads around it. An act of sheer audacity, a radical art for art's sake provocation, MONA catalyzed a potential that had been simmering in the island state for years. It was what the astronomers call an 'event', changing the very configuration of the cultural field, energising and activating a new sense of what living in Tassie could mean. But it seems the state can only begin to comprehend what is happening if it can translate it into the metricised language of overnight stays and inward investment. Five years into a breathtaking reimagining of a place and its people, it looks likely that the most visible impact will be—yes, a waterfront leisure development *on the very site* of one of MONA's key festivals.

It is in this light that we need to value initiatives such as Renew Newcastle, which attempted to 'hack' the existing property, development and planning settings to get creatives into empty spaces in Newcastle's CBD on short term licences. After decades of planning stalemate people actually began creating and making in this historic city's CBD. As with the reform of the ABC or the arts funding system, we need a knowledge of the real workings of the economy of these sectors in order to secure public value from them. It is this understanding not just of 'the market' but of the social, political and cultural underpinnings of this market that I prefer to call cultural economy, and it is only with this knowledge that the cultural values that are central to that economy can be secured. It is the task of public policy to concern itself with these values, and we need to begin a robust argument for them before the very space for such an argument is closed down.

This might sound ever overly pessimistic so let me conclude by reframing what is at stake. I will use two quotations. The first comes from an academic writing about the landscape of contemporary culture:

> *Art is closer to people than at any other time in history. People make and compile music. They design interiors and make-over their bodies. They watch more television and more movies. They think deeply about food and clothes. They write software and surf the net of music videos and play on-line games together. They encounter, study, learn and evaluate languages, diasporas and heritages. There is also a massive daily practice in the arts, from underground music, to making gardens, to creative writing camps ... There is a massive daily register of judgment, critique, attention, and taste.*[25]

On the face of it, this is a realisation of Schiller's dream of the creative society. But is there a dark side? What if all this becomes—as it does in the creative industries argument—an economy occupied with efficiency and cost-effectiveness, vulnerable to monopoly players providing culture at the right price? In this vision, we have a recipe for the collapse of culture into individual consumer preference; one of those efficiently provided entertainment systems that used to go by the name *panem et circenses.*

Culture was always about the collective too. In his recent John Peel lecture, the composer Brian Eno spoke about culture as 'synchronisation', as something that takes the form of 'drills, dances, and parades'. In a fast-moving and complex world, where nobody knows everything, even everything about their own little field, 'we need ways of keeping in synch, of remaining coherent'.

> *Culture is a sort of collective ritual, or a set of collective rituals that we are all engaged with...It's nice to know we have contributed £28 billion ... to the gross national product...The most important thing [however] is that we have all been together—that doesn't just mean the artists... it means everyone. It means all the people actually in the community, everybody—has been generating this huge, fantastic conversation which we call culture. And which somehow keeps us coherent, keeps us together.*[26]

Eno paints a picture of a post-scarcity society, where robots will do all the work, and we will finally have plenty of time for creative self-realisation. 'We are going to be even more full-time artists than we are now.' Would I really be shouted down if I said that our current political direction points not to a liberation from work, but to unemployment, austerity and a general sense of human redundancy? The new possibilities that surround us are immense. But if we remain focused, like Plato's cave-dwelling prisoners, on the flickering economic metrics on the wall rather than how we are actually making our living in the real world, we will remain chained to those illusions of growth and prosperity which never yet managed to make us feel more secure or happy.

What is at stake in culture—as has always been, though we frequently forget it—are the great questions of ultimate value: of how we can live together and what the quality of our collective experience should be. These have not disappeared in an age of cultural abundance. They are even more urgent, as the possibility of a truly human creative society is in one way more realisable, in another as far away as it has ever been.

Endnotes

1 John Hartley 'Creative Industries ' in Hartley, J. (Ed) *The Creative Industries* (Oxford: Blackwell, 2005), p.19.

2 Stuart Cunningham, *What Price a Creative Economy?* Platform Paper 9 (2006), p. 4.

3 For an excellent account see Melissa Nisbett et al., *Culture, Economy and Politics: the case of New Labour* (London: Palgrave Macmillan, 2015).

4 Pierre Bourdieu, *Distinction: a social critique of the judgement of taste* (London: Routledge, 1984).

5 Ernst Bloch, *Heritage of Our Times* (Cambridge: Polity, 1991).

6 See World Commission on Culture and Development, *Our Creative Diversity* Paris: UNESCO, 1996.

7 Scott Lash & John Urry, *Economies of Signs and Space.* (London: Sage, 1994).

8 'The creative industries in the UK generate revenues of around £112.5 billion and employ some 1.3 million people. Exports contribute around £10.3 billion to the balance of trade, and the industries account for over 5% of GDP. In 1997–98, output grew by 16%, compared to under 6% for the economy as a whole'. What these figures are actually measuring is a moot question. DCMS, *Creative Industries Mapping Document 2001.* Department of Culture, Media and Sport. (London: HMSO, 2001). Executive summary. https://www.gov.uk/government/uploads/system/uploads/attachment_data/file/183544/2001part1-foreword2001.pdf

9 DCMS ibid. 'Executive Summary.'

10 John Howkins, *The Creative Economy: how people make money from ideas* London: Penguin, 2001.

11 Richard Florida, *The Rise of the Creative Class* (New York: Basic Books, 2002).

12 Douglas McWilliams, *The Flat White Economy. how the digital economy is transforming London and other cities of the future* (London & New York: Duckworth Overlook, 2015).

13 Hasan Bakhshi, Alan Freeman & Peter Higgs, *A Dynamic Mapping of the UK's Creative Industries.* (NESTA, 2012), online at http://www.nesta.org.uk/publications/dynamic-mapping-uks-creative-industries.

14 'In sociology and economics, the *precariat* is a social class formed by people suffering from precarity, which is a condition of existence without predictability or security, affecting material or psychological welfare' *Wikipedia.*

15 See Justin O'Connor and Mark Gibson, *Culture, Creativity, Cultural Economy: a review* (ACOLA, 2015) online at http://acola.org.au/PDF/SAF01/6.%20Culture%20creativity%20cultural%20economy.pdf
16 EU Commission (2010) Green Paper: *Unlocking the Potential of Cultural and Creative Industries, http://cdc-ccd.org/IMG/pdf/CEDC_Contribution_ICC_Green_Paper_28-7-2010_final.pdf*
17 *2009 UNESCO Framework for Cultural Statistics* (Montreal: UNESCO Institute for Statistics, 2009), online at http://www.uis.unesco.org/culture/Pages/framework-cultural-statistics.aspx
18 Creative Victoria's Creative Industries Strategy can be found at: http://creative.vic.gov.au/Projects_Initiatives/Creative_Industries_Strategy
19 Nick Feik, 'The Start-up Whisperer: just how innovative is the Turnbull government's innovation package?', *The Monthly,* March 2016.
20 Department for Culture, Media and Sport , *Connectivity, Content and Consumers: Britain's digital platform for growth* (London: DCMS, 2013) online at https://www.gov.uk/government/publications/connectivity-content-and-consumers-britains-digital-platform-for-growth
21 O'Connor and Gibson, *Culture, Creativity, Cultural Economy.*
22 Tariq Ali, 'Corbyn's Progress' *London Review of Books* 38 (5) (March 2016), p. 22.
23 Costas Lapavitsas, *Profiting without Producing: how finance exploits as all* (London: Verso, 2013).
24 Colin Griffith, 'Share or merge? Public not well served by an ABC monopoly', *The Mandarin* 8 March 2016, online at http://www.themandarin.com.au/61508-mark-scotts-friendly-merger-abc-sbs-monopoly/?pgnc=1&pgnc=1
25 Stefano Harney, 'Unfinished Business: labour, management, and the creative industries', in M. Hayward (ed.), *Cultural Studies and Finance Capitalism* London: Routledge, 2012, p. 156.
26 Brian Eno's John Peel Lecture was given September 2015; online at http://www.bbc.co.uk/programmes/p033smwp

Copyright Information

PLATFORM PAPERS
Quarterly essays from Currency House Inc.
Founding Editor: Dr John Golder
Currency House Inc. is a non-profit association and resource centre advocating the role of the performing arts in public life by research, debate and publication.

Postal address: PO Box 2270, Strawberry Hills, NSW 2012, Australia
Email: info@currencyhouse.org.au Tel: (02) 9319 4953
Website: www.currencyhouse.org.au Fax: (02) 9319 3649

ISBN 978-0-9924890-8-3
ISSN 1449-583X

Typeset in Garamond
Printed by McPherson's
Production by XOU Creative

FORTHCOMING

PP 48, August 2016
WHEN THE GOAL POSTS MOVE
Ben Eltham

In May 2015 the Federal Arts Minister, George Brandis, dropped a bombshell on the arts sector. He had deducted $1.05 billion over four years from Australia Council funding and transferred it to his Ministry for distribution at the Minister's discretion. His aim was to provide more 'excellence' and to do away with 'mediocrity'. This act divided the arts like nothing since the Fraser Government in the 1980s brought down ceiling funding on the recently-created State arts organisations at a similar time of stringency. Brandis' action favoured the classic arts but threatened the country's developmental arm, the 'small to medium' sector, and drove a wedge between the two which promised the death of innovation. Journalist and social commentator Ben Eltham traces his coverage of these twelve months: the shocking impact, the actions taken; and asks: How have the arts become so marginalised? Is this the end of our most imaginative initiatives? Of the Australia Council itself? Eltham ruminates on intended and unintended consequences.